Royal Mint Collector Coins

The story behind the 2007 collection

Royal Mint Collector Coins

The story behind the 2007 collection

PUBLISHED FOR THE ROYAL MINT
BY JEREMY MILLS PUBLISHING LIMITED

Royal Mint
Llantrisant, Pontyclun CF72 8YT, United Kingdom.
www.royalmint.com

First published 2006.

ISBN 978–1–905217–20–5

Published by Jeremy Mills Publishing Limited for the Royal Mint.

Jeremy Mills Publishing Limited, The Red House,
22 Occupation Road, Lindley, Huddersfield, HD3 3BD.
www.jeremymillspublishing.co.uk

Designed and typeset by Paul Buckley.
Printed by SNP (International) Limited.

Contents

Contributors

Diamond Wedding

Jim McCue is a journalist, editor and publisher, and currently a visiting research fellow at the Institute of English Studies, University of London. He spent 15 years at *The Times*, latterly as Deputy Obituaries Editor. His Bibliomane column for book collectors covered auctions, scholarly and fine press publishing, libraries and many other subjects. He also runs the Foundling Press, which has published new or neglected material by T. S. Eliot, William Empson, Ben Jonson and A. E. Housman.

Act of Union

Christopher A Whatley is Professor of Scottish History at the University of Dundee, where he is also Vice-Principal and Head of the College of Arts and Social Sciences. He is also a Fellow of the Royal Society of Edinburgh. His most recent publication is *The Scots and the Union* (Edinburgh University Press, 2006); previous books include *Scottish Society 1707–1830: Beyond Jacobitism, towards industrialisation* (Manchester University Press, 2000), and *The Industrial Revolution in Scotland* (Cambridge University Press, 1997).

Slavery

James Walvin is Professor Emeritus of History at the University of York. He has written widely on modern British social history and on the history of slavery and the slave trade. Currently he is historical curator for the parliamentary exhibition on the abolition of the slave trade, 1807–2007. His recent books include, *An Atlas of Slavery* (Pearson/Longman, 2006), *The Slavery Reader*, co-authored with Gad Heuman, (Routledge, 2003) and, for 2007, *A Short History of Slavery* (Penguin) and *The Trader, the Owner and the Slave* (Cape).

Scouting

Anna Sargent graduated with a First in English from the University of Aberdeen and went on to study for a PhD on the works of Rudyard Kipling at the University of Glasgow. Her researches led her to the archive of the Scout Association where the use of Kipling's *Jungle Books* in *The Wolf Cub's Handbook* revealed the connections between the writer and Robert Baden-Powell, founder of the Scouting movement. Anna Sargent became the first female editor of the Scout Association's national magazine (2000–05) and now focuses on special projects relating to Scouting heritage. Her co-authored book, *An Official History of Scouting*, was published in 2006.

Foreword

Collector coins issued by the Royal Mint play a distinctive role in commemorating important events and anniversaries, and in so doing they become in their own way national symbols. Our intention through the chapters of this book is to offer collectors of United Kingdom coins a sense of the history that lies behind the themes of the several coins being issued in 2007. It is a wonderful way of revealing the thought that goes into the preparation of new coins and provides an opportunity for us to introduce to collectors the artists who have been inspired to create coinage designs of lasting merit.

Her Majesty The Queen and His Royal Highness The Duke of Edinburgh will celebrate their Diamond Wedding anniversary in November 2007 and the Royal Mint will be issuing a crown piece bearing a specially-commissioned conjoint portrait of the royal couple. The writer and publisher Jim McCue has prepared a thoughtful account of their life together that is full of insight into their characters and that highlights their devotion not only to their public responsibilities but also to each other.

Three hundred years ago the Act of Union joined Scotland and England together politically and the Royal Mint is marking the anniversary with the issue of a two-pound coin. Drawing on extensive research in which he has been engaged for several years, Professor Christopher Whatley of Dundee University has written a scholarly essay on the political context in which the Union emerged. Also falling in 2007 is the bicentenary of the abolition of the slave trade within the British Empire and a two-pound coin will be released to commemorate this crucial step on the path to the complete abolition of slavery. Distinguished historian Professor James Walvin skilfully unravels the story of the key role that the popular protest movement played in eventually bringing about a change in the law to abolish this trade in human lives. On the fifty pence piece, it is the centenary of the Scout Association that is being celebrated and we have commissioned Anna Sargent, author of a recent official history of Scouting, to write about the movement's origins and how it has developed from humble beginnings under the legendary Robert Baden-Powell to a worldwide organisation embracing millions of young people.

Chapters have also been included which focus on the one pound coin, the sovereign and a new design for the Britannia bullion coins, all accompanied by the thoughts of the artists alongside related historical introductions.

To my mind modern commemorative coins are about bringing the history of Britain into people's everyday lives and the delight I have had in reading this book is in knowing it will play a part in communicating the beauty and relevance of modern British coinage.

David Barrass
DEPUTY MASTER (CHIEF EXECUTIVE)

Double Portraits on the Coinage

The crown piece of 2006 commemorating the Diamond Wedding of the Queen and Prince Philip is one of only a handful of British coins to bear a double portrait. In recent times conjoint effigies have been used on two other crowns issued to celebrate royal occasions, namely the marriage of the Prince of Wales and Lady Diana Spencer and the Golden Wedding of the Queen and Prince Philip. It is necessary to go back a few hundred years, however, to find examples of this type of design on British coins intended for general circulation.

The first English coins to bear a double portrait were issued during the reign of Mary I after her unpopular marriage to Philip of Spain. Although regal power remained vested in the Queen, Philip's effigy was included on issues of shillings and sixpences. The two portraits were shown facing each other after the style of the gold coins of Ferdinand and Isabella of Spain produced half a century earlier. In keeping with the conventions of a male-dominated society, Philip was afforded the primary position to the left of the design despite his lesser constitutional status.

Coins of Mary's reign continued to circulate until the Great Recoinage at the end of the seventeenth century. The apparent affection between the royal couple as depicted on the coinage moved the English poet, Samuel Butler (1612–80), to write the following epigram:

Still amorous, and fond, and billing Like Philip and Mary on a shilling.

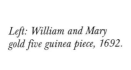

Left: William and Mary gold five guinea piece, 1692.

Scottish gold ducats followed shortly afterwards which included the effigies of the royal couple. A very limited number of pieces was struck and only a few are now known to exist. Following the death of Francis in 1560, Mary decided to return to her native Scotland. The ill-fated marriage with Henry, Lord Darnley took place five years later and a small number of silver ryals bearing facing portraits was issued into circulation. Francis and Henry both appeared to the left in their respective double portraits, conveying the same sense of masculine precedence as in England.

It was more than a century before the Glorious Revolution resulted in the next example of a double portrait on circulating coins. In 1688 a group of notable English Protestants invited William of Orange to invade and secure the succession for his wife Mary, the Protestant elder daughter of James II. William landed at Torbay on 5 November and, after a brief period of uncertainty, James II fled to France. It was widely believed that Mary alone would assume the throne but, having come this far, William had no intention of accepting

Such romantic sentiments were far removed from those Protestant contemporaries who suffered at the hands of Queen Mary. Bishop Hooper was burned at the stake in Gloucester on 9 February 1555, and his widow would later describe the portraits on the coins as 'the effigies of Ahab and Jezebel'.

It was not long before the fashion for facing portraits extended north of the border to the independent Scottish coinage. Mary Queen of Scots was brought up at the French Court and in 1558, at the age of 15, was married to Francis, Dauphin of France. An issue of

Mary Queen of Scots and Lord Darnley.

the position of consort. In the face of his threats to return home to the Netherlands, the opposition in Parliament crumbled and on 13 February 1689 William and Mary were declared joint monarchs.

With the accession of two sovereigns, it became necessary to prepare a double portrait for the coinage and this took the form of conjoint effigies rather than the facing type of Philip and Mary. The classical style was in the ascendancy at the end of the seventeenth century and it seems likely the choice of design was derived from conjoint portraits on Roman coins, such as those of Mark Antony and Octavia, and Claudius and Agrippina. Despite the equal status of William and Mary, regal power was exercised almost single-handedly by the King and perhaps for this reason his portrait was afforded the foremost position in the design.

The circumstances surrounding the use of double portraits in early modern Britain serve as a reminder of the intense political manoeuvring associated with royal marriages. Both Philip of Spain and William of Orange married English brides in order to secure military co-operation against France.

The first marriage of Mary Queen of Scots was intended to strengthen the 'Auld Alliance' between Scotland and France, and her second to Lord Darnley, the great-grandson of Henry VII, was motivated by a desire to shore up the claim of her descendants to the English throne. Mary's marriage with Darnley may have been hugely unsuccessful in personal terms but, as hoped for, their son James was destined to become King of England as well as Scotland.

During the sixteenth and seventeenth centuries the use of double portraits in England and Scotland was reserved for Kings and Queens. With the Golden and Diamond Wedding crowns the Duke of Edinburgh has become the first Prince Consort to appear on the British coinage, although the position of prominence has now properly been accorded to the Queen.

The decision to adopt new obverses for both these coins prompted the inclusion of Prince Philip's effigy, resulting in designs which represented the marriage in a more complete manner. After serving for more than 50 years as President of the Royal Mint Advisory Committee, it is perhaps appropriate that he should have been honoured in this way.

Portraits of William and Mary from the Bank of England collection.

Diamond Wedding

Anniversary

The Queen and the Duke of Edinburgh
often take part in celebrations of national
anniversaries. In 2007 the nation is
celebrating one of theirs. By contrast with
the pageantry of the 60th wedding
anniversary of the Queen and the Duke of
Edinburgh, most Diamond Weddings are
private affairs. Only immediate family
and a few friends are usually involved. Yet
because families are of such importance to
the Queen, couples reaching this
milestone have, throughout her reign,
received a message of congratulation from
her. Every such message is a public
recognition of the lasting importance of
marriage, and of the importance of lasting
marriages. As affirmations from the head
of state to the heads of families, they also
symbolise the way the nation is formed of
a family of families.

Diamond Wedding Anniversary
by Jim McCue

Now that it is the turn of the Queen and the Duke of Edinburgh to celebrate their own Diamond Wedding, thousands of messages will be received at Buckingham Palace. There will be official greetings from all around the world, of course, but more significant will be the cards and letters, emails and bouquets from ordinary people, showing a reciprocal appreciation of a long and remarkable

Princess Elizabeth married Lieutenant Philip Mountbatten on 20 November 1947 at Westminster Abbey.

marriage. During their six decades together, the Queen and the Duke have touched the lives of thousands of people; yet many who have never met them will send messages too, partly to congratulate them on their personal anniversary, but also in tribute to a lifetime's thoughtful and purposeful work.

Of all the couples who married in 1947 – still a rather austere time as Britain recovered from the Second World War – few can have had much idea of what was in store for them. For Princess Elizabeth and her fiancé, however, the path ahead was clear. The Princess knew that at some future date, on the death of her father, King George VI, she would become Queen and devote herself to a busy official and ceremonial life. Her husband would, for a time, continue his career in the Royal Navy, but he would also accompany her on important occasions at home and on her many state visits and tours. He would undertake royal duties of his own as well, so that the monarchy could be represented at a wider range of national and international events.

The Queen and Prince Philip riding in a carriage at Royal Ascot, 1969.

The couple had met first in 1939, when Philip Mountbatten, as he was then, was Senior Cadet at Dartmouth. On a visit to the Naval College, the Princess played croquet with him on Captain's lawn – the first of many hoops they would have to go through. Though the handsome cadet was nearly five years older than the Princess, they were soon friends, and over the next few years friendship developed into love.

Shortly after Princess Elizabeth's 21st birthday, the royal engagement was announced, and the day before the wedding, the bridegroom was created Duke of Edinburgh by the King. Like his bride, he was a direct descendant of Queen Victoria and Prince Albert. Even though Albert had died at just 42 and might have done much more, he was a useful example to the Duke of how the consort of a monarch could evolve his

The royal family pictured in 1972.

own role while respecting the limits of his position.

The wedding took place in Westminster Abbey on 20 November 1947, and was broadcast by the BBC, bringing the country some much-needed cheer. The couple then took up residence at Clarence House. However, during the first six years of their marriage, the Duke was often stationed in Malta with the Royal Navy. For a period between 1949 and 1951 his wife lived there with him – the only time she has ever lived abroad.

Amid their many commitments, they were determined to maintain a genuine home life, and they have always been devoted to their four children, the first of whom, Prince Charles, was born in 1948. In some respects, public pressures have probably brought the royal family closer, because only with each other can they truly let down their guard.

Before Prince Charles was even three, his parents undertook their first major overseas tour together, visiting both Canada and the United States in 1951, when they travelled 10,000 miles in just 35 days. It was while they were in Kenya on a second tour, the following year, that Elizabeth learnt she had become Queen.

She was crowned on 2 June 1953 once again in Westminster Abbey. It was a solemn occasion as well as a national celebration, enhanced by the news that morning that a British team had conquered Everest for the first time. The Queen had personally authorised filming of the rituals of dedication, against some advice, so millions were able to witness her Coronation Oath.

Gradually, over the decades, the formality of the monarchy was to soften a little, as the Queen, the Duke and then their children travelled about, meeting more and more kinds of people. There had always been royal links with the services, and these were strengthened when the Duke was given the rank and titles of Admiral of the Fleet, Field Marshal and Marshal of the Royal Air Force, as well as Captain-General of the Royal Marines, in 1953. With his great curiosity about people, though, he wanted to be informed about other sides of national life. So in 1956 the Queen and the Duke began to host informal lunch parties, mixing half-a-dozen guests at a time from different vocations.

All members of the royal family are patrons of many charities, artistic and cultural bodies and the like. But beyond this the Duke wanted to encourage young people specifically to be of service to others and to develop their initiative and skills. So he established the Duke of Edinburgh's Award, which now operates in 100 countries, and which celebrated its 50th anniversary last year.

Changes in the nation are sometimes highlighted by royal events. For instance, the Queen's Silver Jubilee in 1977 was celebrated with street parties across Britain, not very different from the celebrations for VE-Day in 1945. By the time of the Golden Jubilee, the focus of the celebrations had come home to

Buckingham Palace, where a classical concert and a pop concert were staged in the grounds. For the first time, members of the public could join a ballot for entry to the gardens, where thousands enjoyed a picnic and free champagne. When Brian May played 'God Save the Queen' on the roof of the Palace, the move towards a participatory monarchy seemed complete.

The Queen at the 1980 Windsor Horse Show congratulating Prince Philip on his carriage driving.

Most people in Britain today have known no reign other than the Queen's, and cannot remember back as far as the wedding itself. The Queen and the Duke may well reflect that it is not only policemen who are getting younger, but Prime Ministers too. When Elizabeth II came to the throne, her first Prime Minister, Winston Churchill, was 77. Her 10th, Tony Blair, was born during her reign and was only 43 when he took office. To him, as to most of us, the Queen and the Duke of Edinburgh have been reliably ever-present figures, lending continuity and stability even as everything else in the world seems to change. There have been difficulties, of course, and the Duke has occasionally salted proceedings with his wry sense of humour, yet for more than two generations they have carried out their duties with sensitivity and dignity.

They never appear hurried, and yet at one time the Queen took on more than 500 official engagements a year. Keeping

Walkabout after the Jubilee church service at St George's Chapel, Windsor Castle.

Royal Ascot procession, 2004.

up requires extraordinary stamina and resolve. In this, the Duke's support has been crucial, and the Queen has regularly paid tribute to him. Indeed for a time the words 'My husband and I' were often used by satirists. In 1972, however, she deftly turned the tables when she spoke at a lunch in London's Guildhall on the occasion of her Silver Wedding. 'I think everybody will concede,' she began, 'that on this of all days, I should begin my speech with the words 'My husband and I'.' And after huge applause she continued 'We – and by that I mean both of us.'

Their life is perhaps not one that many people would choose, and the Queen and the Duke themselves scarcely chose it. What they did choose was one another. Fortunately for us all, the bright hopes of those who gathered in Westminster Abbey on that November day 60 years ago have been richly fulfilled.

Designer of the Obverse – Ian Rank-Broadley

Ian Rank-Broadley FRBS studied sculpture at Epsom School of Art and the Slade School of Fine Art. Parallel to his studio career, devoted to figurative sculpture, he has maintained an interest in relief sculpture that has resulted in a long association with the Royal Mint. Landmark works for the Mint include his royal effigy, which has appeared on United Kingdom and Commonwealth coinage since 1998, his centennial crown for Queen Elizabeth The Queen Mother and his popular Golden Jubilee commemorative crown of 2002.

Currently Ian Rank-Broadley is engaged on a commission for the Armed Forces Memorial comprising 15 figures, which will form the centre-piece of the United Kingdom's largest war memorial since the Second World War.

The Inspiration

Being granted the privilege of separate private sittings at Buckingham Palace with both Her Majesty The Queen and His Royal Highness The Duke of Edinburgh, allowed me to observe them both at close quarters.

I had worked initially from photographs, executing a plaster model 10 inches in diameter. Observations, drawings and notes made during the sittings enabled me to refine these images and clarify them further.

To experience the easy and relaxed conversation of the Queen and the Duke gave me the opportunity to observe the animation and expression of their faces. It was this that allowed me to achieve portraits that are records of individual humanity in addition to my task of continuing the iconography of royalty.

Designer of the Reverse – Emma Noble

After gaining a HND in general illustration Emma Noble went on to achieve a BA(Hons) at Swansea Institute of design. On graduating in 1997, she joined the Royal Mint as an apprentice engraver undertaking in a two-year training programme. She has worked on an array of coin and medal projects for the United Kingdom and also for several countries throughout the world.

Whilst she has had previous success with her design for the Northern Ireland Prison Service Medal, the 2007 Diamond Wedding crown is her first United Kingdom coin.

The Inspiration

With the more obvious elements already used on previous royal coins and the conjoint portrait to be featured on the obverse, I needed to look elsewhere for my inspiration. I therefore decided to look back to the beginning of the marriage, to Westminster Abbey, where the actual wedding took place. I started by preparing sketches of several features of the Abbey, but then became more focused on the rose window.

For me it was the one element that stood out more than any other and was easily recognisable as part of the Abbey. My final submission of designs make use of various aspects of the rose window, taking certain features and experimenting with different compositions. The design finally selected was the complete window which is quite simple yet visually powerful.

Obverse Design – Ian Rank-Broadley

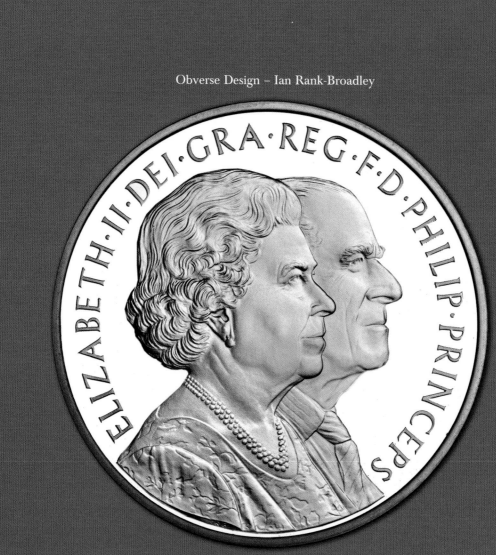

Coin Specifications – The Diamond Wedding Crown

Alloy	Platinum	22 Carat Gold	Sterling (.925) Silver	Sterling (.925) Silver	Cupro-nickel
Diameter (mm)	38.61	38.61	38.61	38.61	38.61
Weight (g)	94.20	39.94	28.28	56.56	28.28
Edge	Plain	Plain	Plain	Plain	Milled

An edge inscription will feature on the precious metal coins: MY STRENGTH AND STAY

The Act of Union

The Union of the English and
Scottish Parliaments that gave birth
to the United Kingdom of Great
Britain has now been in place for
300 years. It has its critics, but when
the Union was forged in 1706–07 it
united the Scots with England in
the then war against a powerful
France. Over the centuries it has
been continuously adapted to meet
the needs of the time.

The Union of 1707: 300 Years On
by Christopher A Whatley

On 1 May 1707 in London's St Paul's Cathedral, William Talbot, Bishop of Oxford, preached a weighty sermon on the advantages of unity between peoples. His words were directed towards Queen Anne, who was also present.

For most of those there – as well as the massed crowds on the streets outside – the Act of Union had come as a blessed relief. Despite being bound together in 1603 by the Union of the Crowns, during the years preceding 1707 relations between the two nations had deteriorated to the extent that armed conflict was seriously considered. The Union removed the immediate cause of inter-national tension – the unwillingness of the Scots to go along with the English Act of Settlement of 1701, which had decreed that Anne's successor should be the Protestant Electress of Hanover, Princess Sophia.

The second of the 25 Articles of Union not only resolved the succession but also debarred 'Papists' from taking the imperial crown of Great Britain. Article III incorporated the Parliaments of

Portrait of Queen Anne.

Scotland and England into one. The united state, declared Talbot, would not only bring peace at home, but also 'riches and plenty' and 'safety from enemies abroad'.

His audience would have been acutely aware of the significance of this last remark: the international context in which the Union was forged was one in which British forces and those of her allies were locked into a lengthy war with Catholic France, a formidable enemy under Louis XIV, whose vision was of a French universal monarchy.

There were Scots who shared in England's joy. A few – the Duke of Queensberry and John Clerk of Penicuik – were in London at the time, basking in the public's adulation. Queensberry, the Queen's Commissioner in Edinburgh, had, with the assistance of men like the Duke of Argyll and the Earls of Mar, Marchmont, Seafield and Stair, steered the Articles through the Scottish

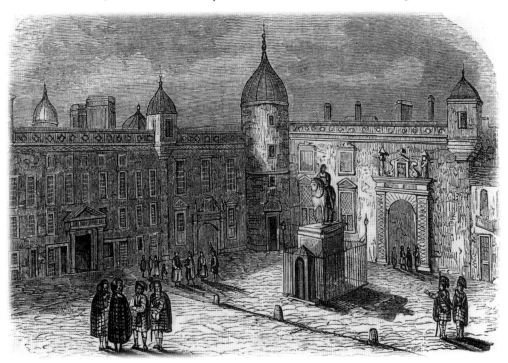

Parliment House and Square, Edinburgh.

Parliament. Clerk's role had been less public, but he was one of a number of Scottish MPs who recognised how parlous Scotland's pre-Union financial condition was, and concluded that incorporation with England offered the best remedy – provided that the Scots could negotiate access to England's colonies, a long-held ambition. This, and the compensation won for the investors in the Company of Scotland Trading to Africa and the Indies who had lost fortunes after the collapse of the

Company's attempt to establish a Scottish trading colony at Darien near the isthmus of Panama, were powerful inducements for Scottish politicians. Inside and outside Parliament the pro-Union cause had been supported too by moderate Presbyterians. Union could secure the gains of the Glorious Revolution of 1688–89 in Scotland. Not only did they fear France and the Church of Rome, but also the return to Scotland of the Stuarts whose king, James VII (II of England), had lost his crowns at the Revolution. Several hundred Scottish Presbyterians had been driven into exile under the later Stuarts. It was from the ranks of the Scots émigrés that calls for an incorporating union had come from Scotland in 1689. Several of those involved were to be amongst the firmest supporters of the Union in 1706–07. To varying degrees too there was amongst the Scottish élite an emergent sense of Britishness: the mood was captured by William Aikman, the Scots-born portrait painter who was in London during May 1707 and informed his uncle that, 'we are no more Scots and English but all bold Brittains'.

Yet Scots who favoured an incorporating union were in a minority; the preference was for a federal system but many thousands opposed further union of any

A view of Panama at the time of the Scottish Darien expedition.

sort. This was particularly so in the south west of Scotland, the stronghold of militant Presbyterianism – the Covenanters – whose leaders wanted no truck with a Westminster Parliament which had a place for prelates. These objectors were men and women who remained committed to the Solemn League and Covenant (1643), for whom closer union with England was contrary to God's purpose: their role was to bring Anglican England within the Presbyterian fold.

Those most hostile, however, were the Jacobites, determined to block a move that would settle the succession on the house of Hanover. They were campaigning in fertile ground. Anti-English sentiment was rooted in the national psyche. Popular heroes were men like Robert Bruce and William Wallace, part-mythical defenders of Scottish independence. Variants on the stirring words of the Declaration of Arbroath of 1320 – 'as long as a hundred of us remain alive, we will never be subjected to the lordship of the English' – were adopted by parliamentary opponents of the Union. Even pro-Union politicians like John Clerk felt uncomfortable about surrendering Scotland's parliamentary independence, although the pragmatic Clerk was persuaded that Scotland's Parliament was impotent in an age of muscular mercantilism: Acts supporting Scottish manufactures and trade were of little consequence without a strong navy to protect Scottish merchant shipping on the high seas, or secured markets abroad.

However, that in the early years of the eighteenth century even English naval vessels had seized Scottish merchantmen had increased animosity towards England; the nemesis was reached in April 1705 when three Englishmen from the crew of the *Worcester*, an English merchant ship taken by the Scots, were hanged on Leith sands. But what had enraged the Scots most had been William III's failure to support the Darien venture: this, the most ambitious colonial scheme ever launched from Scotland, collapsed for many reasons, but it was William who was blamed by most. From the end of 1699 Scottish nationalist feeling reached new heights. Henceforth, Scots who accepted government posts from the London-based monarch were denounced – at best – as unpatriotic.

*Half-crown of 1707 struck at the Mint in Edinburgh bearing the **E** mintmark below the bust of Queen Anne.*

But despite the popular mood, indeed partly because of it and concerns over where the growing animosity between the peoples of the two nations might lead, influential politicians in both countries began to look more favourably towards political union.

Nest of Mint weights prepared at the time of the Act of Union in 1707 and known to later generations as Queen Anne's Pile.

So too had William towards the end of his life for much the same reason and Anne followed suit, with considerable enthusiasm. In many cases Scottish politicians, who defied popular opinion outside Parliament by pushing for the Union, could reasonably claim to be as patriotic as their critics: to them incorporation looked the best way of ensuring that Scotland continued to be Protestant in religion, at peace with its better-off and stronger southern neighbour, protected from its adversaries and more prosperous.

The practicalities of merging the two countries' administrative systems, including the coinage, weights and measures and taxation, proved more difficult than expected. Economic benefits promised to and anticipated by the Scots were slow to materialise. Over time, however, the Union was made to work to the Scots' advantage. Together the peoples of the United Kingdom forged the British Empire and in the nineteenth century established Britain as the 'workshop of the world'. With measures of devolved government implemented for Scotland (and Wales) at the last century's end, the evolving Union still remains intact after 300 years.

Reverse Designer – Yvonne Holton

Born in Aberdeen in 1959, Yvonne Holton studied Jewellery and Silversmithing at Edinburgh College of Art where she obtained an Honours Degree. Throughout her student years she won a number of design competitions before becoming a freelance designer in precious metals. In 1993 she began her career as a book illustrator which led to her joining a small team of heraldic artists and calligraphers used by the Court of the Lord Lyon to illuminate documents. The Office of the Lord Lyon is centuries old and is the chief heraldic authority in Scotland. More recently she has been appointed as the Herald Painter or principal artist in the Court.

The Inspiration

I had only a rudimentary knowledge of this period in the nation's history. My research included reading detailed history books, visits to the Royal Scottish Museum in Edinburgh as well as having the benefit of putting questions to two historians. The thistle and rose, whilst common, are instantly recognisable and relevant symbols as emblems of their respective countries. Similarly, the portcullis to represent Parliament is also easily understood. Therefore, in order to give both countries the same weight in visual terms, the coin had to be quartered. It was not until I was clearing out a cupboard that I discovered my husband's collection of jigsaws. The puzzle pieces are perfect in creating a very effective linking theme between the elements of the coin as well as acknowledging the marriage that the Act of Union represented.

Reverse Design – Yvonne Holton

The obverse design features Ian Rank-Broadley's portrait of the Queen

Coin Specifications – The Act of Union Two-Pound Coin

Alloy	Inner 22 carat yellow gold Outer 22 carat red gold	Sterling (.925) Silver Outer plated with fine gold	Sterling (.925) Silver Outer plated with fine gold	Inner Cupro-nickel Outer Nickel-brass
Diameter (mm)	28.40	28.40	28.40	28.40
Weight (g)	15.97	12.00	24.00	12.00
Edge	Plain	Milled	Milled	Milled

An edge inscription will feature on the two-pound coin coin: UNITED INTO ONE KINGDOM

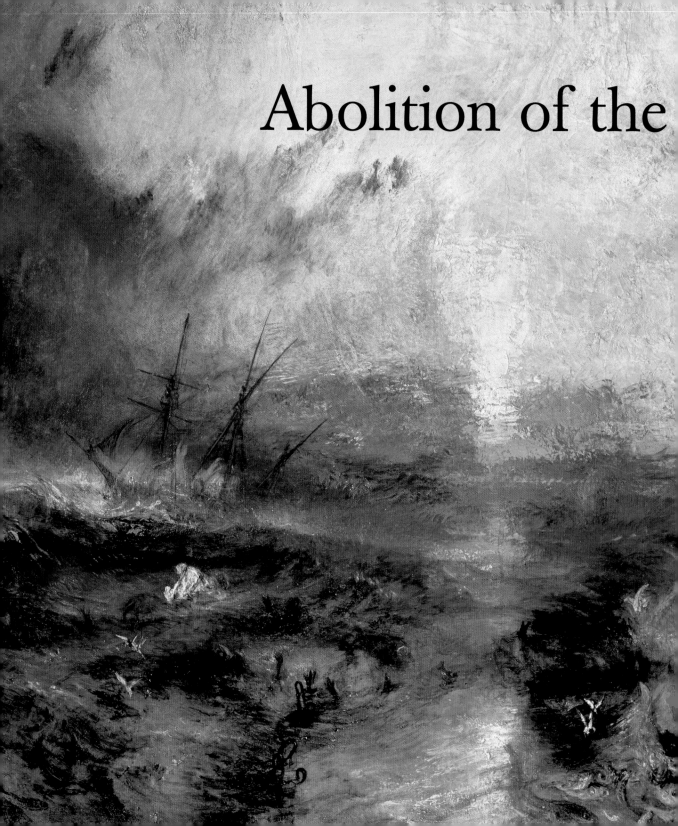

Abolition of the

A remarkable story of popular politics, of changes in economic interests, and of a persistent parliamentary campaign. No one person, obviously, brought about the abolition but without the persistence and doggedness of a small band, as well as the slave resistance in the Caribbean, it is hard to see how abolition could have been effected as and when it took place. The key to abolition was that the British people had turned against the slave trade and it was their pressure which finally persuaded an initially-reluctant Parliament to act. The outcome was the abolition of the slave trade in 1807.

Abolishing the Slave Trade
by James Walvin

The parliamentary abolition of the slave trade in 1807 brought about one of the most dramatic changes ever produced by an Act of Parliament. The British did not initiate the Atlantic slave trade (Spain, Portugal and the Dutch led the way) but in the course of the eighteenth century Britain came to perfect and dominate it. The key to the trade was sugar. Developed first in Brazil, then in the Caribbean islands, sugar production was labour intensive and, from its beginnings, there were never enough indigenous peoples, or European migrants (free or indentured) to provide the necessary workforce. Europeans, however, had begun to use Africans as slaves in the Atlantic islands and they realised that Africa could provide the answer to their labour problem in the Americas. From such small beginnings the slave trade spread – from sugar, to tobacco, later rice and finally cotton in the nineteenth century. By about 1750 enslaved Africans worked throughout the Atlantic economies, with the great majority being transported to work in the sugar fields. Sugar transformed the tastes of the western world as well as the face of Africa and the Americas.

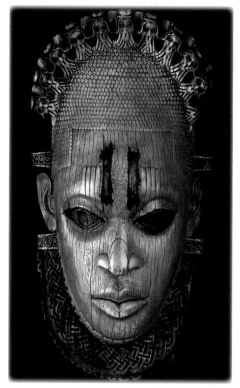

Fifteenth century ivory mask from Benin. Sophisticated cultures flourished in Africa before the arrival of Europeans.

In the region of 12 million Africans were loaded onto the slave ships, with about 10.5 million landing in the Americas.

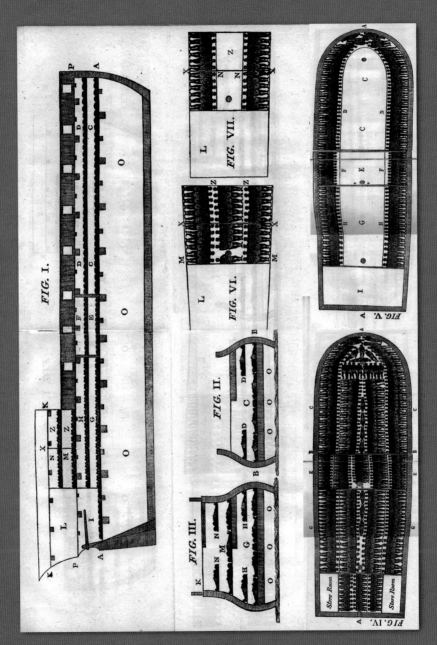

The cross-section of the slave ship Brookes *showing the crammed conditions on board.*

Slaves working on a sugar plantation.

Some 70% were destined, initially at least, to work on sugar plantations and hence the majority of Africans were shipped to Brazil and the West Indies. We know of more than 30,000 slave voyages. London was always crucial, both as a slave port and also as a centre of finance and commerce for the African trade, but it was ships from Bristol (before 1750) and thereafter from Liverpool which dominated the British trade. Many other smaller ports, however, were keen to join in; who today would think of Poole, Workington, Lyme Regis or Preston despatching ships to Africa to trade for slaves? Each outbound vessel was filled with local and regional goods to trade and exchange on the coast for African slaves. It was a lucrative business which attracted investors and backers across the country but for many years it did not attract criticism.

There had been early complaints from religious quarters about African slavery. Critics, led by Quakers, found their voice drowned by the noise of successful commerce but all that changed, quite suddenly and unexpectedly, after 1783 when a number of factors converged to lay the groundwork for the end of the slave trade. There was growing anger, expressed especially by Granville Sharp, about slavery in England itself. Local slave cases stirred the conscience, while Quakers, especially from Philadelphia, continued to speak and write against slavery. But it was the American War of Independence (1776–1783), with its ideology of freedom, which began to unravel the fabric of slavery - despite the fact that the Revolution's leaders were slave owners. The defeated British retreated from America in the company of ex-slaves who had fought on their side and many of those freed slaves joined the ranks of London's black poor. The debate began in earnest: what sort of system had brought this about?

Gradually a small but influential group of Quakers and Evangelical Anglicans came together to campaign against the trade. Their views were promoted by William Wilberforce in Parliament and by Thomas Clarkson who embarked upon extensive lecture tours, recruited support and collected data about the slave trade. Using well-oiled national Quaker networks, the early abolitionists began to publicise grim details about the slave ships.

The Prime Minister, William Pitt, was sympathetic to abolition initially, and agreed to a parliamentary inquiry. The result was a Committee of the Privy Council which listened to dozens of witnesses who had seen the trade at first hand: sailors, traders, ships' doctors all told the same horrifying story. It became clear that whatever profits had flowed from the slave trade came with monstrous suffering amongst the African victims. The evidence was indisputable. Crowded slave decks were reduced to stable-like squalor (especially in bad weather) and the sick and the dead were left unattended as the crew would struggle to sail the vessel. Africans were

Slaves being forced below deck on a ship crossing the Atlantic.

in a state of rebellious despair and violence was never far away; they tried to escape, overpower the crew - or, *in extremis*, fling themselves overboard. It was also clear that a huge number of sailors died, mainly on the African coast from ferocious local diseases. Though the traders tried not to pack the Africans too tightly, and were keen to transport them to the slave markets of the Americas in a healthy condition (it was after all aimed for profit), the environment was such that losses and suffering were inevitable. It was a hellish, brutal trade.

To strengthen their case, the early abolitionists formalised a Committee for the Abolition of the Slave Trade (1787) and called for a national petitioning campaign. The outcome was staggering. The initial push saw 100 petitions, signed by tens of thousands, flood into Parliament. Manchester's alone was signed by more than 10,000 men and women. In London, leaders of the local African community added their voice to abolitionists' demands. Quite suddenly, it was a hugely popular issue. It was steered, initially at least, by local churches and chapels, notably by the increasing ranks of nonconformists whose new chapels were sprouting up across the face of Britain. The country

In the early 1790s hundreds of thousands of people boycotted sugar which had been produced by slaves.

was undergoing major urban and industrial change, and this 'new Britain' found what it learned of the slave trade unacceptable. Although it strengthened their case in Parliament, abolitionists in London were taken aback by the widespread support they received.

Abolition, however, faced a well-organised opposition. The West India lobby, representing all the slave-based interests from planters to shippers, had long been able to bend the ear of statesmen and politicians. After 1787, however, the abolitionists had secured the moral high ground and they began to poke holes in the economic arguments of the slave interests. Not only did the slave trade appear wrong, perhaps it did not even make economic sense. This argument, already advanced by Adam

Smith, was promoted by Thomas Clarkson on his lecture tours where he carried African goods and produce to show what a normal trade with Africa might yield. It was also promoted by the African, Olaudah Equiano, whose autobiography of 1789 was a major black contribution to the abolitionist case. If the slave trade was wrong and uneconomic - why not abolish it?

A campaigning banner calling for the end to the apprenticeship system, which operated between 1834 and 1838.

The abolition cause was delayed, however, by manoeuvres in Parliament and government. It was especially damaged by the impact of the French Revolution and by the massive slave upheaval in Haiti. Britain's consequent disastrous attempt to seize Haiti cost 40,000 British lives. The calamities of the 1790s seemed to confirm what the West India lobby had always said; tinker with the slave system and anarchy would follow. Abolitionists won some small improvements, including a reduction of the numbers of Africans allowed on slave ships and the compulsory presence of doctors. But it was to take major political reform, a brief peace with France, and a change of government (Pitt had turned against the movement) before Parliament passed the Abolition Act. An illegal Atlantic trade, prosecuted by the Royal Navy, continued, mainly to Brazil and Cuba, and was not finally ended until the 1860's. But in 1807 Britain had changed tack dramatically. The greatest slave trader of the eighteenth century became the major abolitionist power of the nineteenth.

Reverse Designer – David Gentleman

David Gentleman RDI is a water-colourist, illustrator, wood-engraver and lithographer whose designs have ranged in scale from a platform-length mural on the London Underground to many stamps for the Royal Mail. He has also written and illustrated books on Britain, London, Paris, India and Italy.

His 2005 coin commemorating the Entente Cordiale was issued simultaneously by the Royal Mint and by the Monnaie de Paris.

The Inspiration

The Mint's brief was very specific: to commemorate not the abolition of slavery itself but a more limited yet crucial step in that direction, namely the 1807 Act which effectively abolished the slave trade within Britain and its colonies.

While looking for a graphic way to suggest this theme, I found that most of the historic images were about slavery itself. Many were vivid representations of noble but miserable African victims. However, these did not specifically represent the trading of slaves.

My design therefore celebrates the salient effect of the 1807 Act symbolically, as release from subjection represented by a break in the chains of oppression.

Reverse Design – David Gentleman

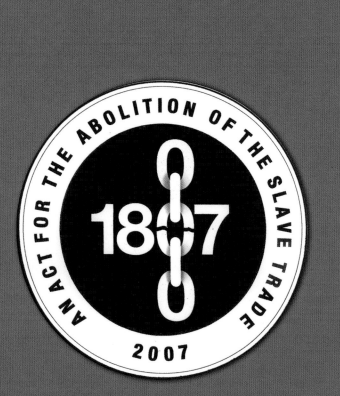

The obverse design features Ian Rank-Broadley's portrait of the Queen

Coin Specifications – The Abolition of the Slave Trade Two-Pound Coin

Alloy	Inner 22 carat yellow gold Outer 22 carat red gold	Sterling (.925) Silver Outer plated with fine gold	Sterling (.925) Silver Outer plated with fine gold	Inner Cupro-nickel Outer Nickel-brass
Diameter (mm)	28.40	28.40	28.40	28.40
Weight (g)	15.97	12.00	24.00	12.00
Edge	Plain	Milled	Milled	Milled

An edge inscription will feature on the two-pound coin coin: AM I NOT A MAN AND A BROTHER
Specimens of the abolition of the slave trade two-pound coin were not available in time for publication.
The artist's original design is shown above.

Scouting

Centenary

Considering that there are now 28 million Scouts worldwide, and nearly a million people involved in Scouting in the United Kingdom alone, you might be forgiven for imagining that Scouting was more than 100 years old. However, 2007 is a year of worldwide celebrations of the Scout movement's 100th birthday.

From the first experimental camps, starting with 20 boys, Robert Baden-Powell inspired young people all over the world to take to the outdoors, and take part in life. His favourite image of the little acorn growing into the great oak has come to fruition and goes on growing. Just as an oak is considered young at 100 years old, so Scouting looks and feels young because of its constantly renewing membership and its focus on adventure, active citizenship and international friendship.

Scouting Centenary
by Anna Sargent

When he was eight years old, Robert Stephenson Smyth Baden-Powell wrote himself a list of 'laws for me when I am old'. He cannot have imagined, even in his wildest dreams, that 28 million young people would be following in his footsteps in 2007.

Sometimes it seems that Scouting has always existed, and that it is an intrinsic part of growing up in Britain. It is

Robert Baden-Powell, Chief Scout of the world.

certainly true that it has become an identifiable aspect of British culture, but Scouting really belongs to the world. Each of the member countries (and only six nations do not have a recognised Scout organisation) sees Scouting as part of their own national identity in just the same way. In some countries, it is even part of the national curriculum.

One of the most important factors in the development of Scouting, in Britain and worldwide, was the personality of Baden-Powell himself. Born in 1857, his almost ruthless determination to succeed, coupled with his considerable charm and adventurous spirit, produced a national hero and an inspirational leader of young people.

His involvement in the siege and relief of Mafeking during the Anglo-Boer War (1899–1902) propelled him to the front pages of newspapers worldwide. His face and upright soldierly stance were depicted on commemorative china, alarm clocks and thousands of other household items and collectables, and he was to stay in the public eye for the rest of his life, swapping his military uniform for a Scout uniform along the way. After a brief period during which he was involved in setting up the South African Constabulary, 'B–P' returned home in search of a new direction and adventure.

Thousands of children wanted to emulate their hero, who had helpfully produced a fascinating military handbook entitled *Aids to Scouting for NCOs and Men*, full of instructions on drill and personal training. This publication rapidly became an unofficial handbook for training in boys' clubs, and it came to the notice of Sir William Smith, founder of the Boys' Brigade, who asked Baden-Powell to work on a programme for a younger, civilian audience.

This was the beginning of Baden-Powell's new life. Whilst he was still officially involved with military matters in Britain, Ireland, Egypt and the Sudan, the seeds of Scouting were germinating. He met a number of people who spurred him into setting down his ideas for training and motivating boys, none more influential than C. Arthur Pearson, publishing magnate and charitable benefactor. Pearson's 'Fresh Air Fund', designed to get children from the crowded cities out into the country for exercise and fresh air, was a vital

A souvenir alarm clock showing Queen Victoria surrounded by the heroes of the South African campaigns – B-P is at 'four o'clock'.

influence, and his expression of interest in publishing Baden-Powell's ideas was absolutely vital to the success of the early Scout movement. B-P tested his principles at an experimental camp on Brownsea Island, Dorset, in 1907 using 20 boys from very different backgrounds in the first patrols, and through this camp Scouting was born.

Scouting for Boys was first published by Pearson in 1908 in six fortnightly instalments, and then as a collected volume, along with a boys' magazine called *The Scout*, which survived until 1966.

Pearson also offered Baden-Powell an office in central London and members of his own staff as support. What had started as a guide for existing youth organisations was becoming a successful movement with its own identity. Pearson was aware of its significance to his publishing empire, but the nation was even more certain of its importance.

Girls were not to be excluded from the fun, and the Guide movement was soon to follow. 10,000 girls were 'Girl Scouts' by 1909, and many were present when Scouts gathered at a rally at the Crystal Palace in London that year. Baden-Powell was glad of his sister Agnes's support in the early days of Girl Guiding, which was officially founded in 1910.

The first volume of the first serial edition, Scouting for Boys, *1908*

'Experimental' Scouts make a bracken mattress, Brownsea Island, 1907

Under her leadership it developed its own separate momentum and identity, and was particularly encouraged by Baden-Powell's wife, Olave, when she took over the reins from Agnes, becoming Chief Guide in 1918. Olave remained devoted to Girl Guiding until her death in 1977.

Scouting soon started to take root overseas, initially in British territories and dominions across the Empire and then further afield. Scouting was particularly suitable for mission or church-based youth groups. Faith and 'duty to God' were strong components in Scout Law, and still are, but Baden-Powell was careful not to limit the movement relevance to the Christian faith alone.

Belief in God, as far as he was concerned, was an extension of right-mindedness – a concept of duty and obedience in an everyday civilian context came from an appreciation of a duty to the highest authority possible, but he was not specific about the theology of the faith itself. Scouting was therefore as attractive to church-based youth groups in need of a programme as it was to youth groups in different contexts and different countries.

The first decade, 1907–1917, saw the greatest expansion of Scouting, geographically and numerically, slowing only at the onset of the First World War. Cub Scouting began in 1916, adding younger boys. However, both world wars had significant impacts on Scouting, its numbers and its ethos. Initially, the movement had received a great deal of support from military and naval establishments who saw Scouts as ideal recruits, and it was certainly true that Scouts who joined the forces were often promoted quickly as a result of their previous training and their attitude to service. Thousands of former Scout leaders, Scouts and former Scouts, were active in the various services during the First World War, and thousands lost their lives.

However, Scouting was principally about citizenship, and after the 'war to end all

A smart salute from a troop of female Scouts, 1909

A six of Cub Scouts preparing dinner at camp, c.1920.

wars', the emphasis of the Scout movement worldwide was re-affirmed. 'Do your best' may have meant one thing in wartime, but it was something very different in peacetime, the point of Scouting as a worldwide movement being to promote peace through bonds of friendship.

The movement lost Baden-Powell in 1941 and, while this was felt personally and deeply, the continuation of Scouting was not in question. It had come to represent a principle of freedom and international friendship that was worth fighting for. The Jamboree for Peace, held in 1947 (after a 10-year wait), was populated by young people who had seen death at first hand. Despite food rationing, a war-ravaged host country and a severe lack of resources, the French held an event to which young people came in the hope and expectation of peace in their time.

Since then, the focus of the worldwide movement has been on creating and keeping those international bonds alive through joint ventures and communications, co-ordinated through the World Organisation of the Scout movement, now based in Geneva. On a day-to-day level, however, Scout groups in member nations get on with the business of encouraging and enabling young people to flourish and to discover their roles in a wider society. The emphasis on responsible citizenship has not changed – only the way in which it is expressed.

No barriers for girls – an increasing proportion of Scouts are female.

As well as the ceremonial duties they perform at the Annual Service of Remembrance and on other state occasions, Scouts from the United Kingdom have taken part in many home-based and overseas community projects. Scouting and Guiding organisations have been jointly responsible for some of the most important international projects in peer education, offering health screening and information on HIV/AIDS, leprosy, malaria, hygiene and other vital subjects to young people.

They have also helped provide shelter, education and first aid to children in deprived parts of the world and those areas affected by natural disasters.

In the main, however, the business of Scouting is about the development of an individual into an active team player, through outdoor activity, adventure, and by stretching their horizons. Scout leaders are still volunteers, and Scouting depends on the energies and resources of those adults able and willing to spend their own time on training and leading activities. Without them, Scouting would be impossible, but where such people can be found, Scouting thrives, and the movement is set fair to survive another 100 years.

Reverse Designer – Kerry Jones

Kerry Jones completed her BA (Hons) in Applied Arts at Derby University in 2000. After graduating she worked in the field of interior design for several retail companies. In 2004 she began her career as an engraver at the Royal Mint and has since worked on a number of coin and medal design projects. During her first year as a trainee she was awarded a commendation in the Goldsmiths' Crafts & Design Council Awards.

In the summer of 2005 she was invited to enter the competition to design the reverse of the 2007 Scouting fifty pence, and much to her delight her submission was successful. This is her first United Kingdom coin.

The Inspiration

The briefing for the Scouting fifty pence competition was held at Gilwell Park in Chingford, the headquarters of the Scout Association. All the invited artists who gathered there for the meeting received a warm welcome and were given details of the extensive work in which Scouts are involved.

I was inspired by the creativity, simplicity and the sense of adventure that Scouts promote. To my mind the official logo – the Fleur de Lys – had to be the dominant part of the design. The image is symbolic of the four points of a compass and is instantly recognisable, as is the Scout's famous motto 'Be Prepared'.

The depiction of the globe emphasises the growth of the Scouting organisation and how important it has become all around the world.

The obverse design features Ian Rank-Broadley's portrait of the Queen

Coin Specifications – The Scouting Fifty Pence Coin

Alloy	22 Carat Gold	Sterling (.925) Silver	Sterling (.925) Silver	Cupro-nickel
Diameter (mm)	27.30	27.30	27.30	27.30
Weight (g)	15.50	8.00	16.00	8.00
Edge	Plain	Plain	Plain	Plain

The Gold Sovereign

The evolution of St George and the Dragon

Over the course of the last 200 years the classic portrayal of St George and the Dragon by Benedetto Pistrucci has become a symbol of continuity and stability on the gold coinage. In the early years of its existence, however, the design underwent a number of revisions and it took two or three years to arrive at the composition with which we are familiar today.

The sovereign was introduced in 1817 and, given its proximity in size to the guinea, there were concerns that a conventional heraldic reverse could lead to confusion. Pistrucci's design of St George and the Dragon was chosen as an alternative and represented a marked break from British numismatic tradition. In this earliest treatment, the features of which are rather heavy, St George is shown holding a shattered lance in his right

hand, another portion of which is lodged in the body of the dragon.

A crown piece was struck a year later and a decision was made that St George should appear on the reverse.

Right: Sovereign of 1817.

Attempts were made to produce enlarged copies of the sovereign design using a mechanical three-dimensional copying machine. The process was found to be too technically challenging and instead a new punch had to be prepared from scratch.

Pistrucci, ever the perfectionist, seized upon the opportunity to improve on his earlier work and the revised version was intended in every respect to be a masterpiece, capturing the power and poise of the neo-classical spirit. St George was now shown with a sword and he appeared to be mounting a second attack because the broken lance still protruded from the side of his adversary. At the beginning of the reign of George IV the designs on the sovereign and crown were brought into line with one another. The general treatment followed the crown of 1818 but a square-beaded border replaced the Garter and the helmet was shorn of its streamer.

While the date had previously appeared on the obverse, it was now inserted in the exergue below the figure of St George. Pistrucci and his work fell out of favour and in the mid 1820s St George was replaced by the Royal Arms on both the sovereign and crown. The design remained unused until 1871 when it was revived by Charles Fremantle, Deputy Master of the Mint, as part of his attempts to improve the quality of numismatic art and his initiative was not in vain. St George has appeared on every sovereign struck since the Jubilee coinage of 1887, with the exception of three special issues in the last 20 years.

The streamer was restored to St George's helmet in 1887 and further revisions followed, including the removal of the initials of William Wellesley Pole, Master of the Mint from 1814 to 1823. Pole, an elder brother of the Duke of Wellington, took great pride in introducing the new sovereign in 1817 and was keen to have his name associated with it, even to the extent of having the letters WWP included on the reverse. One imagines he would have been satisfied to know that by the time his initials were dropped they had appeared on millions of coins circulating in every corner of the globe.

With the first coinage of George IV, the revised version of St George and the Dragon had largely achieved its modern form. It was Fremantle, however, who recognised the greatness of Pistrucci's work and but for him the world's most famous coin design could have remained simply a footnote of British numismatic history.

The obverse design features Ian Rank-Broadley's portrait of the Queen

Coin Specifications – The Sovereign Coins

Denomination	Five Pounds	Double-Sovereign	Sovereign	Half-Sovereign
Alloy	22 Carat Gold	22 Carat Gold	22 Carat Gold	22 Carat Gold
Diameter (mm)	36.02	28.40	22.05	19.30
Weight (g)	39.94	15.97	7.98	3.99
Edge	Milled	Milled	Milled	Milled

Britannia Gold and Silver Coins
The Changing face of Britannia

Over the course of the last 300 years the image of Britannia on the British coinage has been reinterpreted many times in response to changing political and artistic currents. A variety of symbolic objects and background features have come and gone, and the treatment of Britannia herself has also varied. Through these modifications, changes may be discerned in the way Britain has viewed both itself and the rest of the world.

The Romans used female figures to represent nations which came under their dominion, and Britannia appeared for the first time in the second century AD on the coins of three emperors. After this brief introduction she vanished and it was almost 1,500 years before her image was restored to coins circulating in Britain.

During the seventeenth century the struggle between the Dutch and English for control of the seas erupted into violence on a number of occasions. In 1609 the Dutch statesman Hugo Grotius argued in his book *Mare Liberum* that the seas were free for all nations. The English scholar and jurist John Selden

wrote a response, *Mare Clausum*, published in 1635 in an attempt to prove the British position that the seas were private property. His evidence to support this included Roman coins bearing the figure of Britannia which, he maintained, showed her presiding over the waves.

A generation later in 1665 pattern farthings were produced and, in light of Selden's remarks, a Britannia reverse was prepared by John Roettiers with the inscription QVATVOR MARIA VINDICO, I claim the four seas. When copper halfpennies and farthings were subsequently issued in 1672, the design was retained although without the inscription. A relatively benign figure, Britannia is set in isolation, holding a spear in one hand and an olive branch in the other.

The design remained largely unaltered on copper coins until the end of the eighteenth century. 'Cartwheel' pennies and twopences issued in 1797, however, had a new style of Britannia, drawn it is believed by Nathaniel Dance and engraved by Conrad Küchler. Neptune's

Left: Pattern farthing of 1713 on which Britannia is depicted in a portico.

Cartwheel penny of 1797 struck at Matthew Boulton's Soho Mint.

inclusion of a helmet, however, and the removal of the olive branch was perhaps a reflection of Britain's growing military self-confidence.

Bronze coins were issued in 1860 to replace the heavier copper pieces and Leonard Charles Wyon, the son of William, was responsible for their design. His depiction of Britannia was similar to that of his father's but the sea and ship were restored and a lighthouse was added to the composition. In 1895 the ship and lighthouse were removed, provoking a considerable number of letters of complaint from members of the public. It was not until 1937 that the lighthouse was given a reprieve and it thereafter remained on the penny until the time of decimalisation.

In addition to her long service on the base-metal coinage, Britannia has also made occasional appearances on denominations in silver. An innovative design by George William De Saulles of a standing Britannia was chosen for florins of Edward VII. Her proud and majestic gaze seems to symbolise the imperialist

trident appears in place of the spear, and the figure of Britannia is shown surrounded by waves with a ship in the distance. The new design emphasised even more forcefully the connection between Britannia and the sea, serving as a reminder of the naval power protecting Britain from invasion at the time.

A fresh portrayal of Britannia by William Wyon was introduced in 1825 on the copper coinage and, in keeping with the neo-classical style to remove unnecessary detail, he omitted the sea and ship. The

sentiment that reached its height around the turn of the twentieth century. The new reverse also served the very practical purpose of increasing the ability to distinguish between florins and half-crowns.

Within two generations the British Empire had substantially diminished in size but the figure of Britannia did not lose her ability to command respect and appreciation. When it was revealed in 1968 that she would not appear on the new decimal coins, questions were asked in the House of Commons and a place was soon found for her on the fifty pence piece. The design was prepared by Christopher Ironside and after an absence of nearly 150 years the olive branch was restored, resulting in a

Britannia with a more peaceful air. A lion was shown to the left of the seated figure, in much the same style as it had appeared on the Britannia reverse by William Wyon for the farthings of George IV.

In 1987 Britannia was given a new lease of life with the introduction of the gold bullion coins which bear her name and image. Twenty years on, the design for the coins of 2007 has been prepared by Christopher Le Brun RA. The seated figure of Britannia gazes out to sea, with cliffs disappearing into the background and a lion stretched out at her feet.

Like so many of its illustrious predecessors on the British coinage, the design incorporates traditional symbolism in a contemporary style producing a composition which is both dignified and arresting.

Bronze penny of Victoria, 1861.

Reverse Designer – Christopher Le Brun

Christopher Le Brun RA studied painting at the Slade and Chelsea schools of Art. Following his first one-man exhibition at the Nigel Greenwood Gallery in London in 1980, he established an international reputation exhibiting in many shows, including 'Zeitgeist' in Berlin 1982 and 'Avant-garde in the eighties', in Los Angeles 1987. In 1996 he received a major commission from the Jerusalem Trust for paintings for the choir of Liverpool Cathedral. In the same year he was elected to the Royal Academy where he was Professor of Drawing until 2002.

Christopher Le Brun's work can be found in many public collections in Britain and abroad including the Tate Gallery, the British Museum, the Fitzwilliam Museum and the Museum of Modern Art, New York.

The Inspiration

When I embarked on this project I wanted to find a way to bring my imagination as a painter to bear on the problem of coin design. The emblematic nature of the imagery can be expanded or given leave to return to the original notion of Britannia as the personification or nymph of the islands. I find this very evocative: the figure on the shore of Albion, the wooded island, owing something to the imagery of Spenser and Milton.

I have tried to reward the eye and the mind with something less immediate whilst still fulfilling with clarity the essential purpose. In the end, of course, I have tried to make something that I myself would enjoy returning to look at. It is also (for the child in me) a great opportunity to depict shields and lions. Although familiar, Britannia is a profoundly strange, yet highly emotive image which still remains rich with possibility. The plaster was carved by John Bergdahl based upon my original drawing.

The obverse design features Ian Rank-Broadley's portrait of the Queen

Coin Specifications – The Britannia Coin

Denomination	£100	£50	£25	£10	£2	£1	50p	20p
Alloy	22 Carat Gold	22 Carat Gold	22 Carat Gold	22 Carat Gold	.958 Silver	.958 Silver	.958 Silver	.958 Silver
Diameter (mm)	32.69	27.00	22.00	16.50	40.00	27.00	22.00	16.50
Weight (g)	34.05	17.02	8.51	3.41	32.45	16.22	8.11	3.24
Edge	Milled	Milled	Milled	Milled	Milled	Milled	Milled	Milled

One Pound Coin
Gateshead Millennium Bridge

The introduction of the bridge designs by Edwina Ellis for the one pound coin marked a significant departure for the British coinage. In keeping with this spirit of innovation, it is perhaps appropriate that the series should conclude with a bridge representing the best in modern engineering.

As part of its regeneration plans for the area, Gateshead Council launched a design competition in 1996 for a foot and cycle bridge over the River Tyne to connect Gateshead Quays with Newcastle's thriving north bank. Six entries were short-listed and, after an extensive public consultation exercise, the contract was awarded to Wilkinson Eyre Architects, and structural engineers Gifford & Partners Limited.

The Gateshead Millennium Bridge was built at a fabrication yard six miles downstream from the proposed site.

On 20 November 2000, the 850-tonne construction was transported up the Tyne by the *Asian Hercules II*, one of the largest floating cranes in the world.

Crowds of up to 30,000 people waited to cross the bridge for the first time on 17 September 2001, and it was officially opened by the Queen on 7 May 2002 as part of the Golden Jubilee celebrations.

The total cost of the project was approximately £22 million, part funded by a lottery grant from the Millennium Commission.

An elegant addition to the line of distinguished bridges crossing the Tyne, the Gateshead Millennium Bridge has received widespread critical acclaim for the originality of its design. It consists of two arches, one of which serves as the deck while the other provides support through a series of steel suspension cables. To allow shipping to pass underneath, the whole assembly rotates as a single rigid structure in an operation which suggests the opening of a huge eye-lid.

In 2002 it became the first bridge to win the Royal Institute of British Architects' Stirling Prize for Building of the Year, the United Kingdom's premier architectural award.

The bridges that featured on the first three designs of Edwina Ellis's four-year series were built in the nineteenth century and in their different ways helped to define the industrial revolution. By selecting the Millennium Bridge for her final design she has brought the story right up to date and has captured a dramatic perspective of an elegant structure.

Edwina Ellis

The obverse design features Ian Rank-Broadley's portrait of the Queen

Coin Specifications – One Pound Coin

Alloy	22 Carat Gold	Sterling (.925) Silver	Sterling (.925) Silver	Nickel-brass
Diameter (mm)	22.50	22.50	22.50	22.50
Weight (g)	19.62	9.50	19.00	9.50
Edge	Milled	Milled	Milled	Milled

Edge design: symbolising bridges and pathways.

Acknowledgements

Double Portraits on the Coinage

Portrait of Mary Queen of Scots and Lord Darnley from the *Book of Kings* engraving by Renold Elstrack, 1618, courtesy of Bridgeman Art Gallery, p.7.

Full-length portraits of William and Mary attributed to Sir Godfrey Kneller, courtesy of the Governor and Company of the Bank of England, p.9.

Diamond Wedding Anniversary

A profile of Her Majesty The Queen and His Royal Highness The Duke of Edinburgh taken at Buckingham Palace, 2001, by Patrick Lichfield, p.10.

All images in the article by Jim McCue are courtesy of Camera Press, London.

Ian Rank-Broadley photograph, courtesy of the artist, p.18.

The Act of Union

Queen Anne being presented with the Articles of Union, courtesy of the Palace of Westminster, p. 22.

Portrait of Queen Anne, courtesy of the Highland Photographic Archive, p.24.

Parliament House and Square, Edinburgh, courtesy of Mary Evans Picture Library, p.25.

The pages of the Articles of Union, courtesy of Parliament Archives, p.26.

A view of the coast of Panama at the time of the Scottish Darien expedition, courtesy of Mary Evans Picture Library, p.27.

Yvonne Holton photograph, courtesy of the artist, p.30.

Abolition of the Slave Trade

Slave Ship, 1840 by J.W.M. Turner © the Museum of Fine Arts, Boston, courtesy of the Bridgeman Art Library, p.32.

Benin Ivory Mask © Trustees of the British Museum, p.34.

Sugar Bowl © Norfolk Museums and Archeology Service, p.38.

All other images courtesy of Anti-Slavery International. For more information visit www.antislavery.org /2007.

David Gentleman photograph, courtesy of the artist, p.40.

Scouting Centenary

Scouts burst joyfully out of a bell tent, *c.*1929, p.42.

All images courtesy of the Scout Association.

The Gold Sovereign

St George struggling with the Dragon *c.*1503–05, by Raphael of Urbino, courtesy of Bridgeman Art Gallery, p.52.

Britannia Gold and Silver Coins

Christopher Le Brun photograph, courtesy of the artist, p.60.

One Pound Coin

Gateshead Millennium Bridge at night, p.62.

All images in the article © Graeme Peacock Photographic Images.